INTEGRITY RISKS AND RED FLAGS IN
EDUCATION PROJECTS

JANUARY 2023

ASIAN DEVELOPMENT BANK

ADB

Notes:
References in this publication to bidders, bids, bid evaluation committees, and bid evaluation
reports are used within the context of the procurement of works (contractors), goods (suppliers),
and consulting and non-consulting services.

All photos by ADB except when otherwise stated.

In this publication, "$" refers to United States dollars.

On the cover: **Batam State Polytechnic**. Electronics engineering students at this Indonesian
school—a grant recipient of ADB's Polytechnic Education Development Project—design their own
printed circuit boards at one of the campus' numerous electronics labs (photo by Lester Ledesma).

Cover design by Paolo Tan.

CONTENTS

TABLES, FIGURE, BOXES, AND CHECKLISTS

TABLES

FIGURE

BOXES

CHECKLISTS

FOREWORD

Since 2003, the Asian Development Bank's Office of Anticorruption and Integrity has conducted proactive integrity reviews (PIRs) to identify and address control weaknesses that give rise to integrity risks in ongoing sovereign operations. Insights from these PIRs are published in this series, *Integrity Risks and Red Flags*.

This publication highlights weaknesses and red flags identified through PIRs of 10 education projects financed by ADB. Further volumes in the series feature insights from five other sectors: agriculture, natural resources, and rural development; energy; health; transport; and water. Through this sector-based series, governments, public bodies, and stakeholders engaged in designing and implementing projects can learn from past vulnerabilities and establish processes and controls to effectively mitigate integrity risks.

To help foster and sustain economic growth, ADB's Strategy 2030 underscores the strengthening of governance and institutional capacity as an operational priority in the bank's developing member countries. Let us achieve a prosperous, inclusive, resilient, and sustainable Asia and the Pacific by maintaining the highest ethical standards.

John Versantvoort
Head, Office of Anticorruption and Integrity
Asian Development Bank

ACKNOWLEDGMENTS

Integrity Risks and Red Flags in Education Projects was prepared and developed collaboratively by H. Lorraine Wang (former advisor), Caridad Garrido Ortega (former senior integrity specialist and consultant), and Erickson M. Quijano (consultant) of the Preventive and Compliance Division, Office of Anticorruption and Integrity, Asian Development Bank.

This publication greatly benefited from the insights and comments of John Versantvoort (head), David Binns (former advisor), Lisa Kelaart-Courtney (director), Jung Min Han (senior integrity specialist), and Kristopher Marasigan (integrity officer) of the Office of Anticorruption and Integrity. This publication was made possible by reviews from Brajesh Panth (chief of Education Sector Group, Sustainable Development and Climate Change Department) and Alaysa Escandor (public management officer - Governance, Sustainable Development and Climate Change Department).

ABBREVIATIONS

AACT	average annual construction turnover
ADB	Asian Development Bank
BEC	bid evaluation committee
CSC	consultant selection committee
DMC	developing member country
OAI	Office of Anticorruption and Integrity
PIR	proactive integrity review
PMU	project management unit

INTRODUCTION

Since the Asian Development Bank (ADB) adopted its Anticorruption Policy in 1998, fighting corruption has become embedded in ADB's broader work in governance, public administration, and capacity development.[1] The Anticorruption Policy affirms the bank's zero tolerance for corruption and lays the groundwork for supporting anticorruption efforts.

ADB's Strategy 2030 identifies strengthening governance and institutional capacity as one of seven operational priorities for a prosperous, inclusive, resilient, and sustainable Asia and the Pacific. The Office of Anticorruption and Integrity (OAI) promotes the implementation of this operational priority through a combination of activities aimed at (i) enforcement and (ii) prevention and compliance.

The proactive integrity review (PIR) is a mechanism used by ADB since 2003 to help prevent and detect integrity violations and address integrity risks in ADB-financed or -administered projects. PIRs (i) identify and assess integrity risks in procurement, contract and asset management, and financial management of a project; and (ii) recommend measures to mitigate these risks and ensure that project funds are used for their intended purposes.

PIRs evaluate the adherence of projects to three core principles of project integrity: (i) transparency—proper documentation of key decisions, public disclosure of project information, and protection of confidential information; (ii) fairness—objective and reliable bidding process and requirements optimizing competition, impartial evaluation, and a credible complaints mechanism; and (iii) accountability and control—accurate and timely project accounting and reporting, eligibility of expenditures and timely payments, adherence to contract provisions, and adequate project oversight and management.

OAI ensures that PIR knowledge is applied to the projects reviewed through follow-up reviews, at which time OAI verifies the implementation status of the PIR. In addition, OAI assists the executing and implementing agencies in addressing open recommendations.[2]

PIR knowledge is institutionalized in ADB operations through (i) embedding of PIR requirements in ADB guidance and instruction documents, (ii) integrity risk management reviews, (iii) knowledge enhancement and transfer workshops and other learning courses, and (iv) knowledge products.[3] Following a country-focused approach (one of three guiding principles outlined in Strategy 2030), PIR knowledge also informs the country partnership strategies of developing member countries (DMCs).[4] Through this exercise, PIR knowledge is considered in designing new projects as the country partnership strategy predominantly drives country operations business plans.

This publication presents vulnerabilities from PIRs of 10 education projects (Appendix) across 9 countries and 4 regions, and highlights recommended measures to mitigate identified integrity risks.[5]

---

[1] ADB. 1998. *Anticorruption Policy*. Manila.

[2] The follow-up review reports document the implementation status of PIR recommendations (footnote 5).

[3] Through integrity risk management reviews, PIR knowledge is built in preapproval project documents (concept papers, reports and recommendations of the President to the Board of Directors, technical assistance reports).

[4] The country partnership strategy is the primary platform for defining ADB's operational focus in a developing member country.

[5] The education projects reviewed were selected from all active ADB-financed loan and grant projects using a risk-based selection process. The selection process took into account the size of funding, lending modality, implementation arrangements, number of awarded contracts, level of disbursements, input from relevant ADB departments, prior project results, external benchmarking, and potential benefits of a proactive integrity review (PIR) to the project. PIR reports are available on the ADB website (*https://www.adb.org/who-we-are/integrity/proactive-integrity-review*).

SECTOR OVERVIEW

ADB has a long track record in assisting DMCs achieve the goal of quality education for all, disbursing over $14 billion in loans and grants to the education sector over more than 50 years. ADB provides finance and advisory assistance to DMCs for education services to tackle key challenges such as (i) increasing enrollment (access), (ii) improving education outcomes (quality and relevance), (iii) reducing education inequality (equity and inclusiveness), and (iv) reducing costs (finance and cost-efficiency).

Table 1 presents ADB's financial resources commitments in the education sector from 2017 to 2021.

Table 1: ADB's Financing Commitments in the Education Sector, 2017–2021

YEAR	2017	2018	2019	2020	2021
Value ($ million)	723	1,643	1,138	1,066	975
Percent of commitments in all sectors	3.32%	6.70%	4.74%	3.38%	4.28%

Source: ADB. 2022. ADB Annual Report 2021. Manila.

INTEGRITY RISKS AND RED FLAGS

Methodology

OAI identified and synthesized integrity-related vulnerabilities, including red flags, from all its education PIR findings.[6] An integrity-related vulnerability is any gap in a project's implementation processes that, if not remediated in a timely manner, will increase the likelihood of an integrity violation occurring and/or the impact of an integrity violation. In other words, the vulnerability increases the integrity risk profile of the project.

Integrity risk is the risk that project funds are diverted from their intended purposes due to fraud, corruption, or other integrity violations.[7] Integrity violations are more likely to occur if integrity risks are not detected or not addressed effectively in a timely manner. Integrity risk management is an essential prerequisite for ensuring that projects achieve the intended development outcomes.

OAI assessed the level of vulnerabilities (high, medium, or low) by occurrence and impact.[8] This publication follows the project implementation processes and related subprocesses shown in Table 2. This document describes high- and medium-risk vulnerabilities and mitigating measures in each project implementation process.

Table 2: Project Implementation Processes

Process		
Procurement	**Contract and Asset Management**	**Financial Management**

Subprocess		
A1 Bidding Prequalification, bidding documents preparation, bid advertisements, submissions, and opening	**B1 Contract administration** The management of the day-to-day practicalities and administrative requirements under the contract	**C1 Expenditure management** Approval and processing of payments for project expenditures
A2 Bid evaluation Assessment of bidders' compliance with bidding requirements, and preparation and approval of evaluation report	**B2 Output monitoring** Engagement with and/or supervision of contractors, consultants, and suppliers in relation to project outputs	**C2 Financial reporting** Project accounting and auditing
A3 Contract award Post-bid evaluation activities until contract is awarded and signed	**B3 Asset control** Safeguarding and maintenance of project assets including asset inventory	

Note: The subprocesses reflect those prioritized by the Office of Anticorruption and Integrity and do not reflect all subprocesses that exist within each process.

Source: Office of Anticorruption and Integrity, Asian Development Bank.

---

[6] Red flags are indicators of irregularities, which may indicate the occurrence of integrity violations. Project staff should be alert to red flags of integrity violations for them to promptly report potential violations to OAI.

[7] Integrity violation is any act which violates ADB's Anticorruption Policy, including corrupt, fraudulent, coercive, or collusive practice; abuse; conflict of interest; and obstructive practice. Other integrity violations include violations of ADB sanctions, retaliation against whistleblowers and witnesses, and other violations of ADB's Anticorruption Policy, including the failure to adhere to the highest ethical standards.

[8] OAI determined the occurrence of a vulnerability by establishing the frequency with which this was identified in the PIRs; and based the impact of a vulnerability on the likelihood that this could have resulted in an integrity violation or misuse of project funds.

Integrity Risk Heat Maps

The heat map in Figure (a) shows the level of risk arising from the vulnerabilities identified in the education PIRs and presented in the processes in which they manifested.[9] In the 10 education projects reviewed, OAI identified high integrity risks in all processes, i.e., procurement, contract and asset management, and financial management.

Figure (b) shows the risk level by subprocess. Risk levels are highest in bidding (A1), bid evaluation (A2), and expenditure management (C1) subprocesses.

Figure: Integrity Risk Heat Maps

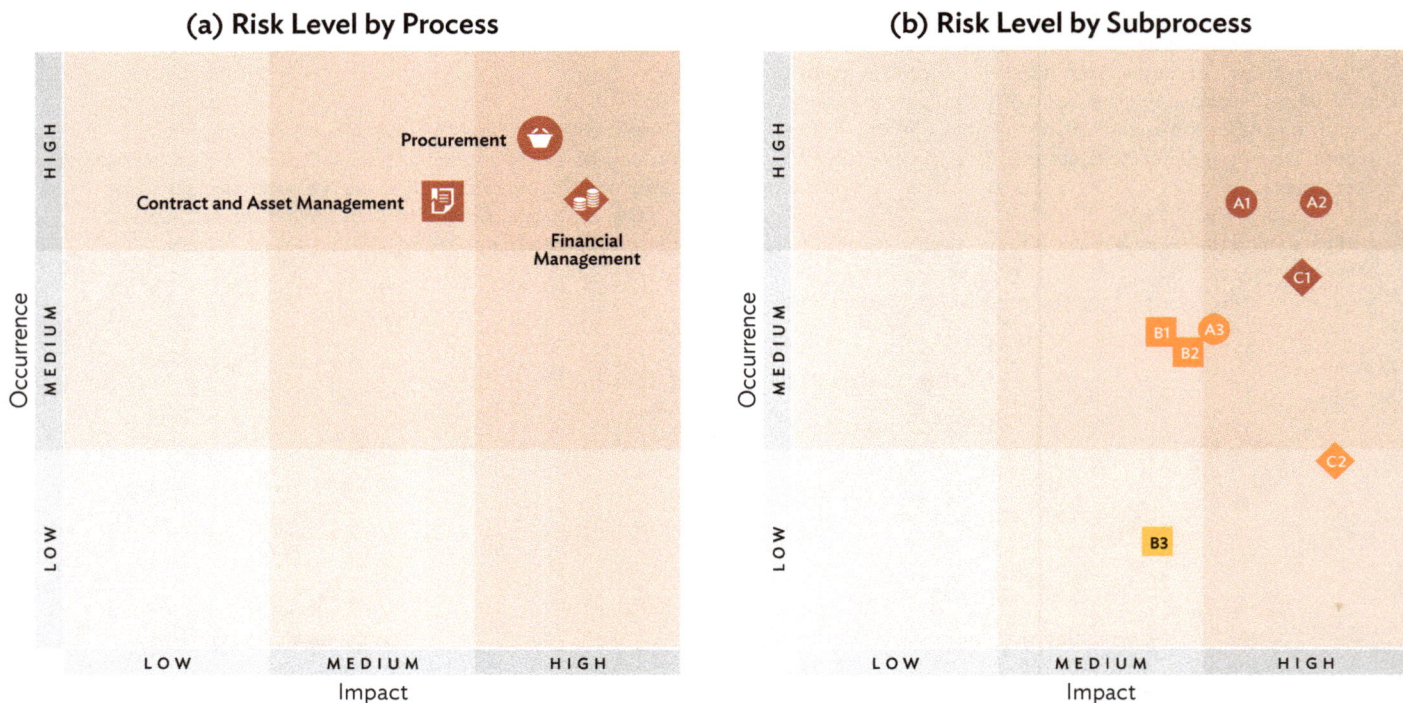

(a) Risk Level by Process

(b) Risk Level by Subprocess

Note: The color of the icons represents the aggregate risk level of the vulnerabilities in each process/subprocess:
high-risk medium-risk low-risk

Legend:

- Procurement
- A1 Bidding
- A2 Bid evaluation
- A3 Contract award
- Contract and Asset Management
- B1 Contract administration
- B2 Output monitoring
- B3 Asset Control
- Financial Management
- C1 Expenditure management
- C2 Financial reporting

Source: Office of Anticorruption and Integrity, Asian Development Bank.

---

9   The heat map is a visual representation of relationships among two sets of data: the likelihood that an integrity violation may occur (occurrence) and its potential impact to the project (impact).

Vulnerabilities and Mitigating Measures

OAI's analysis aimed to identify factors contributing to integrity vulnerabilities and to formulate risk mitigating measures. These measures may be applied to all projects regardless of their financing modality or structure. Project teams can use the due diligence checklists during bid evaluation (Checklist 1) and expenditure payment processing (Checklist 2) to identify and mitigate the risks.[10]

PROCUREMENT

Ⓐ1 Bidding

Red flags of integrity violations. OAI identified red flags indicating that the fairness of the bidding process may have been undermined. These increase the likelihood of occurrence of fraud and corruption occurring that may jeopardize the project and alienate prospective bidders. Examples of red flags in bidding are summarized in Table 3.

Red flags are multifaceted, and those summarized in Table 3 may have one or a combination of the elements of collusion, fraud, corruption, and/or conflicts of interest. Box 1 presents conflict of interest situations.

Box 1: Cases—Conflict of Interest Situation

Close Socialization with an Expert

The executing agency had a very long and productive working relationship with an expert of the firm awarded the project consultancy for the project. This resulted in the expert representing the executing agency in many situations, both on a retainer and volunteer basis.

During the time the project was compiling expressions of interest from project consultancy firms, the expert—as a representative of the chair of the consultant selection committee (CSC)—corresponded with ADB on matters pertaining to evaluation criteria and scoring for shortlisting, and discussed evaluation criteria and scoring with CSC members. This created a conflict of interest for the expert, given his participation in the bidding process as a named expert on a consultancy firm's proposal for the consultancy services contract in question. This may have resulted in the expert being improperly influenced.

TAKEAWAY

A conflict of interest is not always avoidable, and where identified should be adequately managed. The mere appearance of impropriety should be avoided. In this case, the involvement of the expert in the request for proposals process, in discussing and deciding on evaluation scoring with the CSC chair, and in discussing evaluation scoring with ADB, created a conflict of interest. The CSC should not have sought the expert's assistance, and the expert should have recused himself. The expert's advice and actions cannot be assumed to be objective, and this may have compromised the bidding process.

Source: Office of Anticorruption and Integrity, Asian Development Bank.

---

[10] OAI rolled out project management checklists to help executing and implementing agencies to self-assess (i) executing/implementing agency capacity, (ii) project procurement processes, (iii) financial management, and (iv) project output management from an integrity perspective. These checklists are available at https://www.adb.org/who-we-are/integrity/proactive-integrity-review.

PROCUREMENT

CONTRACT
AND ASSET
MANAGEMENT

FINANCIAL
MANAGEMENT

Table 3: Examples of Red Flags in Bidding

Type of Integrity Violation	Red Flags
Collusive practice	**Similarities in bids** • Winning and losing bidders submitted identical bids containing the same financial and technical information, which may indicate that the bids were prepared and submitted by the same entity. • Bids for the same contract package had strong similarities in layout, format, diagrams, and wording. In some cases, spelling and grammatical mistakes were the same.
	Leakage of bid information The joint venture agreement was signed at a date earlier than the bid advertisement date. This indicated the possibility of unofficial access to bidding information by the joint venture.
	Split purchases Considering the proximity of the procurement schedules of three lots and from a procurement perspective, it might have been more economical, efficient, and effective to have procured the three lots under one bidding. Splitting the procurement into three separate lots and three individual procurement exercises appeared to have bypassed the approving authority. Had the three lots been combined in a single procurement package, the aggregate contract amount would have resulted in the referral of the award of the contract to the ADB procurement committee.
Conflict of interest	**Close socialization with contractor/consultant/supplier** An expert, who had a very long and productive working relationship with the executing agency (i.e., representing the executing agency in many situations, both on a retainer and volunteer basis), assisted in the request for proposal preparation for a consultant section. The expert was one of the nominated experts of the winning consulting firm in the selection.
	Contracting personnel failed to disclose conflict of interest A director of a consulting firm who was hired to assist in the bidding activities (including bidding documents preparation) was a key staff member of the winning firm in that bidding.

Notes: 1. Collusive practice is an arrangement between two or more parties designed to achieve an improper purpose, including influencing improperly the actions of another party.

2. Conflict of interest is any situation in which a party has interests that could improperly influence a party's performance of official duties or responsibilities, contractual obligations, or compliance with applicable laws and regulations.

Source: Office of Anticorruption and Integrity, Asian Development Bank.

MITIGATING MEASURES
Red Flags of Integrity Violations

• ADB regional departments and resident missions should ensure that executing and implementing agencies, including project implementing units/offices and evaluation committees, understand their obligations under ADB's Anticorruption Policy, especially the obligation to report any integrity violation to OAI when such allegation is initially identified or suspected. Executing and implementing agencies should communicate these obligations to the bidders (contractors, consultants, suppliers), provide the necessary oversight, and conduct appropriate due diligence to minimize the risk of integrity violations on development projects.

• They should collaborate to ensure that the procurement process is competitive and that the procurement terms are properly evaluated in accordance with ADB's Procurement Policy and Regulations.

• The executing agency should instill tighter oversight on the implementing agency and preclude conflicts of interest with project officials. The executing agency should (i) establish a mechanism to identify and manage perceived or actual conflicts of interest, which might include requiring implementing agency staff to disclose their relationships with contractors/consultants/suppliers; and (ii) actively monitor staff integrity and require staff to adhere to the highest ethical standards.

(A2) Bid Evaluation

Vulnerabilities in bid evaluation can result in contracts awarded to unqualified bidders, thereby undermining the transparency and fairness of the procurement at an ultimate cost to the project. Process inconsistencies and deficiencies, and inaccurate evaluation results may create the impression of favoring bidders. If not addressed, these vulnerabilities may eventually lead to substandard outputs, delayed implementation, waste, loss of funds, or harm to the intended beneficiaries.

Inadequate due diligence. Bidders may provide dubious information on their eligibility, financial capacity, and experience. Without adequate due diligence during bid evaluation, bid evaluation committees (BECs) may fail to identify irregularities, inconsistencies, and/or potential misrepresentation.

Following a risk-based approach, the BEC should conduct due diligence to verify submitted bid information against supporting documents (records check), from online sources (sanctions and other desktop research including previous adverse news), and/or from third parties (reference check). Combined with professional attributes such as a questioning mind and a critical assessment of documents, due diligence requires looking for indications of errors/misrepresentations on the documents, including checking the accuracy of information drawn from computations. The BEC should also seek clarifications/substantiation from bidders to the extent allowed by the bidding documents.

Examples of these evaluation errors resulting from the lack of, or inadequate, due diligence are summarized in Table 4. Box 2 presents sample cases of bid evaluation errors.

Table 4: Examples of Evaluation Errors

Bid Evaluation Aspect/Requirement	Nature of Evaluation Error
Financial capacity	**Working capital and net worth** • The bid evaluation committee (BEC) used the working capital amounts on the bidding forms in a previous bid instead of those of the current bid, which led to the erroneous disqualification of the bidder. Otherwise, the bidder would have been the winner of the bid. • Working capital amounts differed between the bidding forms and the financial statements yet were undetected by the BEC, which resulted in incorrect evaluation of bidder's financial capacity. • The BEC accepted the bidders' unaudited financial statements without first establishing that the law in the bidders' countries/jurisdictions did not mandate financial statements to be audited. **Average annual construction turnover** A computational error caused the BEC to award the contract to a bidder that did not meet the minimum average annual construction turnover requirement. **Credit lines** • The BEC accepted bidders' credit lines that were conditional lines of credit to be made available only if the bidder is awarded the contract, subject to the satisfaction of bank requirements. As such, these were not existing lines of credit readily available to the bidders. • The BEC accepted credit line certificates that were dated a few months prior to the bidding advertisement. ⚠ **Current contract commitments** Bidders, which appeared to be large established companies, indicated zero current contract commitments in their bids which is unlikely, and the BEC did not seek clarification about this questionable information
Pending litigation	The BEC accepted court reference certificates that were dated a few months prior to the bidding advertisement. ⚠

continued on next page

PROCUREMENT

CONTRACT
AND ASSET
MANAGEMENT

FINANCIAL
MANAGEMENT

Table 4 *continued*

Bid Evaluation Aspect/Requirement	Nature of Evaluation Error
Materials	The BEC accepted the winning bidder's proposed construction materials that were not compliant with the bidding requirements. The proposed materials were of inferior quality (in effect cheaper) than those specified in the bidding documents, therefore, resulting in a lower bid price. ⚠

Legend: ⚠ = indicative of potential misrepresentation (fraudulent practice). Fraudulent practice is any act or omission, including a misrepresentation, that knowingly or recklessly misleads, or attempts to mislead, a party to obtain a financial or other benefit, or to avoid an obligation.

Source: Office of Anticorruption and Integrity, Asian Development Bank.

Box 2: Cases—Bid Evaluation Errors

Case 1: Financial Capacity—Credit Lines and Pending Litigation

The bid evaluation committee (BEC) accepted bidders' bank certificates of indebtedness and court reference certificates despite these being dated a few months prior to the bid invitation/announcement. The project implementation unit explained that contractors generally prepare the bid requirements in March or April in anticipation of the bid invitations/announcements for the procurement of construction/civil works contracts being issued in May, for completion prior to year-end. The process starts in May due to harsh weather conditions in the country during the early and latter parts of the year.

TAKEAWAY | CASE 1

Without a third-party verification from the bank and court concerned, the BEC would not be able to determine the applicability of information in the bank certificates of indebtedness and court reference certificates at the time the bidding process started.

Case 2: Financial Capacity—Average Annual Construction Turnover

The BEC committed the following errors in calculating bidders' average annual construction turnover (AACT):

- A bidder's share of the construction turnover in a joint venture where they previously participated should not have been included in the calculation;
- Transposition error (e.g., $1,234,657 value was erroneously entered as $2,134,657 in the AACT computation);
- A losing bidder's AACT was based on turnover figures for an incorrect 5-year period; and

- Incorrect construction turnover figures of a winning bidder were encoded in a worksheet used to calculate the AACT.

TAKEAWAY | CASE 2

Due to errors in calculation of the AACT, BEC may erroneously award the contract to a bidder that did not meet the minimum AACT requirement.

Case 3: Financial Capacity—Current Contract Commitments

Bidders indicated "nil," "none," or "not applicable" in bidding form FIN-4: Financial Requirements for Current Contract Commitments. Particularly for large companies—based on asset size per the audited financial statements and AACT disclosures—the BEC should have questioned such information as part of reasonable due diligence. There was no evidence that the BEC sought clarification from the bidders. In another contract, though a bidder submitted updated information on the FIN-4 form, the BEC used the amount of contract commitments declared by the same bidder in a previous bid for another contract (which the bidder won). The bidder's evaluated contract commitments were, therefore, understated since the amount of the previously won contract was not included in the current commitments.

TAKEAWAY | CASE 3

Undeclared ongoing contract commitments overstate the amount of evaluated available financial resources and could lead to incorrect qualification of an otherwise nonqualified bidder.

Source: Office of Anticorruption and Integrity, Asian Development Bank.

Inconsistent application of bid evaluation criteria. With this, BEC may be perceived to be favoring bidders or being unduly influenced. Examples of inconsistent application of bid evaluation criteria are summarized in Table 5.

Table 5: Examples of Inconsistent Application of Bid Evaluation Criteria

Bid Evaluation Criteria Item	Nature of Inaccurate Information
Financial capacity	The bidding documents required that the bidders' bank balances should be at least 30% of their proposed price. The bid evaluation committee (BEC) evaluated bidders with bank balances lower than 30% of their proposed price and/or that did not submit documentary evidence for their financial capacity as "responsive". On the other hand, the BEC rejected some bids due to the bidders' weak financial capacity though their bank balances were equal to or higher than 30% of their bidding price as required. ⚠
Drawings	The BEC rejected a bid because it did not include required drawings. However, the winning bid also did not include any such drawings. ⚠

Legend: ⚠ = indicative of potential bid manipulation (collusive practice). Collusive practice is an arrangement between two or more parties designed to achieve an improper purpose, including influencing improperly the actions of another party.
Source: Office of Anticorruption and Integrity, Asian Development Bank.

Incorrect evaluation procedure and/or scoring. Similarly, this may give the impression that BEC favors bidders or it is being improperly influenced. Examples of incorrect evaluation procedure and/or scoring are summarized in Table 6.

Table 6: Examples of Incorrect Evaluation Procedure and/or Scoring

Bid Evaluation Aspect	Nature of Incorrect Evaluation Procedure and/or Scoring
Financial capacity	• The bid evaluation committee (BEC) evaluated the bidders' financial capacity based only on the submission of audited financial statements for the last 2 years, instead of evaluating their liquidity (using the acid test or quick ratio) and inventory turnover for the last 3 years, as required by the bidding documents. ⚠ • The BEC did not request from the bidders updated information such as pending litigation, historical financial performance, average construction turnover, and financial resources. These would have a bearing on the evaluation of financial health. ⚠
Sequence of technical and financial evaluation	As indicated in the bidding documents for a procurement package, the bid evaluation should start with the evaluation of technical aspects of the bid (technical evaluation). However, the BEC first compared bid prices and selected the lowest priced bid (financial evaluation). Then, it evaluated the responsiveness of the lowest priced bid to the qualification criteria and evaluated the technical proposal last. In effect, the evaluation process was an exercise of selecting the lowest-cost bidder, rather than selecting the lowest evaluated substantially responsive bidder.

Legend: ⚠ = indicative of potential collusive practice. Collusive practice is an arrangement between two or more parties designed to achieve an improper purpose, including influencing improperly the actions of another party.
Source: Office of Anticorruption and Integrity, Asian Development Bank.

PROCUREMENT

CONTRACT
AND ASSET
MANAGEMENT

FINANCIAL
MANAGEMENT

MITIGATING MEASURES
Vulnerabilities in Bid Evaluation

- BEC members should undergo detailed and practical hands-on training on all aspects of bid evaluation, especially due diligence, before undertaking new bid evaluation assignments. Support from ADB regional departments, supervision consultants, and engaged procurement experts is required (a checklist on how to avoid common errors/lapses in bid evaluation is on Checklist 1).

- ADB regional departments should perform rigorous reviews of bid evaluation reports, particularly when the executing agency's procurement capacity is not robust or when contracts are high value, high risk, or complex. Rigorous review entails seeking clarifications from the executing and/or implementing agencies, calling in bids on a sample basis, validating evaluation report information against bids, and assessing the reasonableness of significant evaluation committee decisions.

Checklist 1: How to Avoid Common Errors and Lapses in Bid Evaluation

ADB Sanctions List

☐ Verify that the bidder (all parties to the joint venture/association/consortium agreement) is not on ADB's complete Sanctions List (https://sanctions.adb.org).

Construction Turnover

☐ Verify the turnover declared on the bidding form against the turnover reported in the audited financial statements submitted.

Financial Capacity

☐ Verify the financial capacity-related accounts (working capital, net worth) declared on the bidding form against the corresponding accounts in the audited financial statements submitted.

☐ Verify the credit lines declared against the supporting documents submitted.

Current Contract Commitments

☐ Verify the current contract commitments declared on the bidding form against the contract commitments reported in the audited financial statements submitted.

Experience

☐ Verify the experience declared in the bidding form against the work completion certificates (for works) and curricula vitae (for experts and consultants) submitted.

Pending Litigation

☐ Verify the pending litigations declared on the bidding form against the pending litigation disclosures in the audited financial statements submitted.

Criteria Requiring Computations

☐ Recompute the amounts on the bidding forms and verify that the formula used, including the exchange rates, are correct.

ADB = Asian Development Bank, OAI = Office of Anticorruption and Integrity.

Note: Where a red flag is identified, refer it to OAI for further verification.

Source: Office of Anticorruption and Integrity, Asian Development Bank.

(A3) Contract Award

Lack of standard accountability provisions in contracts. Failure to include accountability provisions (e.g., audit, anticorruption and records management clauses) in contracts with contractors and subcontractors will make it difficult to verify their compliance with anticorruption, operational, and financial management requirements. These contractual deficiencies result in an inadequate audit trail, thereby making any integrity violations, noncompliance, and other irregularities less detectable.

MITIGATING MEASURES
Lack of Standard Accountability Provisions in Contracts

- The executing agency should use or, if not available, develop with ADB project team's assistance, standard contracts with complete accountability provisions. The executing agency should (i) require the contractors to use this standard contract in hiring subcontractors and (ii) approve only subcontracting contracts with complete accountability provisions.

- The ADB project team should provide or, if not available, jointly develop with the executing agency standard contracts with complete accountability provisions. Before granting no objection to the contract award, the ADB project team should check the completeness of these provisions in the contract.

CONTRACT AND ASSET MANAGEMENT

B1 Contract Administration

Faulty enforcement of contract provisions. Liquidated damages are intended to compensate the project for any delays or losses caused by the contractor or supplier. However, the following faulty enforcement of this penal clause defeated its compensatory function:

(i) The project management units (PMUs) required the suppliers to deposit liquidated damages to the government account rather than deduct these from payments to suppliers as required by the contract. This arrangement created opportunities for the contracting parties to negotiate the terms of settlement of liquidated damages.

(ii) Following (i), ADB replenished the imprest fund based on overstated expenditures since the PMUs claimed for the full amount of the suppliers' contracts without deduction for liquidated damages. In effect, the project was not compensated for the suppliers' delays, since the project funds were used to pay for the full contract amounts.

(iii) Some suppliers with delayed deliveries had received full payments before they paid their corresponding liquidated damages. The delays ranged from 5 to 7 months past the final payments to the suppliers.

(iv) No penalties were imposed on contractors when the civil works were delayed and handover was not made on schedule. In most of these cases, the performance security period was not extended accordingly.

PROCUREMENT

**CONTRACT
AND ASSET
MANAGEMENT**

FINANCIAL
MANAGEMENT

**MITIGATING MEASURES
Faulty Enforcement of
Liquidated Damages**

- The PMUs should monitor expected deliveries and/or completions and closely coordinate with the contractors and/or suppliers to avoid or minimize delays. In cases of delays, the PMUs should promptly impose the corresponding liquidated damages and require the suppliers and/or contractors to deduct the liquidated damages from their claims.

- If the government requires the suppliers and/or contractors to transfer the liquidated damages to the government's account prior to the project financial closure, the executing agency should reimburse the imprest account for all the liquidated damages imposed and collected from the suppliers and/or contractors. ADB project teams should require the PMUs to periodically submit their records of deliveries/completions for appropriate monitoring and reconciliation of reimbursable liquidated damages.

B2 Output Monitoring

Deficiencies in the reporting of project's implementation progress. A lack of transparency in progress reporting results in implementation complications, especially delays and poor-quality outputs, not being addressed in a timely manner. Examples of deficiencies in progress reporting are summarized in Table 7.

Table 7: Examples of Deficiencies in Progress Reporting

Progress Reporting Aspect	Deficiency
Submission of reports	Project implementation units did not prepare progress reports as required by the loan agreement.
Quality of reports	• A quarterly progress report contained internal inconsistencies between the main progress report and the appendixes. • Progress reports did not explain the reasons for contract implementation delays ranging from 5 to 6 months. • Progress reports did not include the frequency of monitoring visits and any follow-up actions made to address issues identified in the visits.

Source: Office of Anticorruption and Integrity, Asian Development Bank.

Use of materials and works that were substandard, defective, or off specifications. Executing and implementing agencies should ensure that contractors are adequately supervised and that any issues are addressed in a timely manner. The PIR asset inspection of education projects identified output defects, deviations from approved designs/specifications, and use of substandard materials, which could have been detected and rectified earlier had the project supervision been more robust. This inadequate supervision of contractors by supervision consultants and executing and/or implementing agencies resulted in delays, acceptance of works that were substandard, and cost overruns. An example of these cases identified by the PIR inspection team are in Box 3.

Box 3: Cases—Use of Substandard Materials and Substandard and/or Defective Works

The constructed school buildings of a project had the following defective works and other quality issues:

- improperly installed roofing sheets and trusses;
- insufficient support from trusses to false ceilings that caused cracked ceiling joints;
- defective plumbing and unhygienic water access points;
- poor electrical works;
- inferior fixtures and fittings in doors, windows, and wash facilities; and
- poor finishing.

Contractors did not set up quality control laboratories at the project sites, in contravention of the contract requirements. The project implementation unit explained that this was not feasible due to the site location. Only a few tests were conducted in a private laboratory due to the difficulties in transporting samples and conducting tests. As a result, the quality of materials used in the construction cannot be ascertained.

The poor quality of works was mainly attributable to (i) weak project supervision, (ii) weak capacity of contractors as repeatedly noted in ADB monitoring reports, (iii) poor quantity and quality control over construction materials and fixtures, (iv) poor workmanship due to lack of qualified workers, and (v) fast pace of construction due to short contract duration (arising from the emergency nature of the project).

TAKEAWAY | CASE 1

Robust project supervision of the civil works contractors enables early detection and immediate rectification of compromised works. In addition, as emergency operations are associated with increased risk of integrity violations, the need for ADB supervision intensifies. This need may be met by more frequent monitoring missions involving a procurement specialist and/or constant supervision by ADB staff in-country.

Source: Office of Anticorruption and Integrity, Asian Development Bank.

MITIGATING MEASURES
Output Monitoring Vulnerabilities

- Erring contractors, consultants, and suppliers should be held accountable to ensure that they fulfill their contractual obligations. This entails enforcing relevant penalty clauses and reporting poor performance to ADB without delay.

- For decentralized, complex, or high-risk projects, independent third-party monitoring firms should be engaged to augment the monitoring activities performed by executing and implementing agencies, ADB regional departments, and supervision consultants.

- Executing and implementing agencies should closely monitor the supervision consultants. This entails enforcing the submission and rigorously reviewing the consultants' progress reports and, as necessary, verification of the progress through field visits. A guide that provides a practical framework for field visits/asset inspections can be accessed through this link: https://www.adb.org/sites/default/files/institutional-document/431571/asset-inspection-project-integrity.pdf.

PROCUREMENT

CONTRACT
AND ASSET
MANAGEMENT

**FINANCIAL
MANAGEMENT**

FINANCIAL MANAGEMENT

C1 Expenditure Management

Ineligible expenditures. Executing and implementing agencies should counter the risk of payments made for ineligible expenditures. Expenditures that are (i) not within the contract terms, (ii) inadequately or inappropriately supported, or (iii) unauthorized are considered ineligible. These indicate that claims were not thoroughly reviewed against contract provisions. They provide opportunities for fraud and expose the project to the risk of loss of funds. Examples of these lapses in expenditure management are summarized in Table 8. Sample cases of ineligible expenditures are presented in Box 4.

Table 8: Examples of Ineligible Expenditures

Expenditure Category	Lapse/Gap in the Expenditure
Transfers to beneficiaries	• Existing documentation could not demonstrate that stipends were paid to eligible trainees or received by these trainees. • Some stipends were (i) transferred to bank accounts not registered in the tracking system, (ii) paid to multiple trainees using the same bank account, and (iii) paid prior to achieving the minimum attendance rate. ⚠
Contractors' progress billings	• Progress payment certificates were not supported by onsite inspection reports and photographs as required by the contract. • Milestone payments were approved even if the advance guarantee had expired and the personnel mobilization requirement had not been complied with.
Suppliers' claims	• The executing agency paid for an invoice despite non-delivery of a significant quantity of goods. ⚠ • The staff who inspected the goods was not authorized to perform such inspection.
Consultants' claims	• Remuneration claims were not supported by timesheets. • The reimbursable expenses to the consultant should be paid at cost based on the contract. However, the expenses were instead paid on a lump sum basis without supporting documents.
Project administration	• Project funds were used to pay the residential monthly telephone bills of a provincial project manager (a retired government official). • Electricity, communication, and travel expenses of the provincial project units were (i) not supported by original source documents, (ii) made without approval, and (iii) not acknowledged by the payees. ⚠

⚠ = indicative of potential misrepresentation (fraudulent practice). Fraudulent practice is any act or omission, including a misrepresentation, that knowingly or recklessly misleads, or attempts to mislead, a party to obtain a financial or other benefit or to avoid an obligation.

Source: Office of Anticorruption and Integrity, Asian Development Bank.

Box 4: Cases—Ineligible Expenditures

Case 1: Transfers to Beneficiaries—Unsupported and Questionable Trainee Stipend Payments

In a skills development project, trainees received stipends after attending 80% of the training classes. Stipends were paid through their bank accounts registered in the trainee tracking system at the time of enrollment.

Nine implementing partner agencies were unable to demonstrate that 68% of the total monetary value of the sample stipends were (i) paid to eligible trainees or (ii) received by these trainees. The following documents were unavailable to verify that the stipends were paid to the trainees: (i) updated list of the trainees' bank account numbers, (ii) certification that the trainees meet the attendance requirement, (iii) bank acknowledgment on the transfer request and/or confirmation on successful transfer of eligible accounts, and/or (iv) trainees' stipend receipt acknowledgment.

Also, there were instances where trainee stipend payments could have been paid to ineligible trainees. This was where (i) payments to bank accounts were not registered in trainee tracking system, (ii) payments to multiple trainees used the same account number, and (iii) proportionate payments were made prior to achieving 80% attendance rate.

TAKEAWAY | CASE 1

Making cash transfers to a large number of beneficiaries poses an increased risk of manipulation because of their small individual values, which allows them to stay "under the radar." As such, it is imperative that the payment eligibility requirements are enforced with their implementation documented for accountability purposes (e.g., future reviews).

Case 2: Suppliers' Claims—Potential Payments Made for Undelivered Goods; Unauthorized Payments

The project management office only examined 10% of computers delivered to the executing agency's warehouse and inspected 10% of installed computers before making payments to the supplier, even though the required sample for inspection was 15%. The project management office should have ensured that all items procured were received before payments were made. Specifically, the warehouse staff should issue inventory certificates for the items received, which are the basis of the payments.

In addition, the inventory certificates documenting the inspections at the warehouse and schools in February and March were signed by an official whose appointment papers were approved only in June. Thus, such inspections were unauthorized.

TAKEAWAY | CASE 2

Procured goods should be inspected by authorized personnel using the set inspection protocols before acceptance and payment to ensure that the goods are delivered at the right quantity and quality.

Case 3: Consultants' Claims—Reimbursable Expenses Erroneously Paid on Lump Sum

Based on the consulting contracts, the project implementation units should pay reimbursable expenses to the consulting firms at cost. However, the units paid them on a lump sum basis without supporting documents. Such expenditures consisted of office rent and running costs, office operations and maintenance, office consumables, rental of vehicles, and communications.

TAKEAWAY | CASE 3

Some expenses are reimbursable at cost because they may be discretionary and thus subject to abuse. As such, the contract provisions on their payment, i.e., that they are only reimbursed at cost supported by documentation, should be enforced.

Source: Office of Anticorruption and Integrity, Asian Development Bank.

PROCUREMENT

CONTRACT
AND ASSET
MANAGEMENT

**FINANCIAL
MANAGEMENT**

🔧 **MITIGATING MEASURES**
Ineligible Expenditures

- Before endorsing claims for payment, executing and implementing agencies should ensure that (i) payment approval procedures are followed, (ii) supporting documents are checked for accuracy and completeness, and (iii) details in the claims are validated against the contracts and supporting documents. Payments should be refused or reduced in line with relevant contractual provisions for works or services

that were not performed or goods that were not delivered. (Checklist 2 shows how to avoid common errors/lapses in expenditure payment processing).

- ADB regional departments and resident missions should ensure that executing and implementing agencies, including project implementing units/offices, understand their obligations under ADB's Anticorruption Policy, especially the obligation to report any integrity violations to OAI without delay when they are initially identified or suspected.

Checklist 2: How to Avoid Common Errors and Lapses in Expenditure Payment Processing

All Types

☐ Verify the claim against the milestone payment terms stipulated in the contract (including contract variations).

☐ Check whether the payment information indicated in the claim matches with the payment information in the contract.

☐ Identify any red flags on the supporting documents submitted, e.g., erasures, alterations, or other errors and ask for clarifications.

Works (Contractors)

☐ Verify the claim against interim payment certificates/certificates of completion. Check if there are claims on non-workdays (work on a weekend or holiday with no preapproval).

Services (Consultants)

☐ Verify the remuneration claim (for input-based contracts) against detailed timesheets submitted.

☐ Verify claims for reimbursable expenses against supporting documents as required in the contract (not applicable for full lump-sum contracts), including:
  ○ Travel costs—proof of travel (tickets, receipts, boarding passes);
  ○ Accommodation—proof of stay (hotel bills, invoices, receipts); and
  ○ Seminars and workshops—attendance sheets, invoices or receipts for workshop costs like venue and equipment rental and refreshments.

Goods (Suppliers)

☐ Verify the claim against sales invoice and delivery receipt/proof that goods have been delivered, inspected, accepted, and, as necessary, properly installed.

OAI = Office of Anticorruption and Integrity.
Note: Where a red flag is identified, refer it to OAI for further verification.
Source: Office of Anticorruption and Integrity, Asian Development Bank.

◇C2◇ Financial Reporting

Inadequate and unreliable accounting systems. To ensure that financial information is provided in a timely and accurate manner for project implementation and progress monitoring purposes, executing and/or implementing agencies should maintain adequate and reliable project accounting systems and apply accounting standards acceptable to ADB. Inadequate and unreliable systems increase (i) the risk of undetected integrity violations, noncompliance, and other irregularities; and (ii) the risk of making an unsound project management decision based on faulty financial information. Examples of accounting systems and procedures deficiencies are summarized in Table 9.

Table 9: Examples of Accounting System Deficiencies

Accounting System Aspect	Deficiency
Financial records	The implementing agencies did not obtain financial records, such as bank statements and expenditure records, from the partner training centers receiving project funds to implement the training activities, i.e., enrollment, training, assessment, and job placement.
Account reconciliations	Reconciliations were not performed between the project and ADB financial records.
Data back-up	The project management office stored the computerized accounting system's back-up on the same computer drive where the accounting system is running, rendering the back-up useless in the event of a computer crash.

ADB = Asian Development Bank.
Source: Office of Anticorruption and Integrity, Asian Development Bank.

MITIGATING MEASURES
Inadequate and Unreliable Accounting Systems

The executing agency should (i) develop appropriate policies and procedures on maintaining adequate and reliable accounting systems, (ii) train all the project management agencies/units/offices on implementing the policies and procedures, and (iii) monitor their compliance with the policies and procedures.

The policies and procedures should include guidelines on maintaining financial records, performing account reconciliations, segregating duties, and accounting procedures for project transactions. For this purpose, the executing agency is encouraged to implement a computerized accounting system, which would facilitate semiautomation of data entry and transactions reviews, and real-time data generation.

CONCLUSION

Through its proactive integrity reviews of 10 education projects, ADB's Office of Anticorruption and Integrity identified vulnerabilities and red flags in (i) procurement, (ii) contract and asset management, and (iii) financial management processes. Key vulnerabilities are summarized in Table 10.

To manage related risks, ADB encourages project staff to apply the mitigating measures recommended in this publication and use the due diligence checklists for bid evaluation (Checklist 1) and expenditure payment processing (Checklist 2). Project staff must remain alert to red flags of integrity violations and report suspected violations to the Office of Anticorruption and Integrity.

Integrity risks are generally elevated in complex, decentralized projects (i.e., large-scale projects involving numerous project components, geographical locations, and implementing entities). These projects benefit from strong accountability and control mechanisms that clarify responsibilities at each implementation level (from the executing agency down to the last implementing unit), and from closer supervision by the executing agency and ADB. Integrity-related controls should be embedded in contracts, manuals, and other authoritative documents.

Under Operational Priority 7 of Strategy 2030, ADB has committed to support governments in their efforts to eradicate corruption and to implement anticorruption measures in all its projects and programs. We trust that the insights compiled in this publication will contribute to these endeavors.

Table 10: High- and Medium-Risk Vulnerabilities in Education Projects and their Implications

Process	Subprocess	Vulnerability	Risk Implication
Procurement	**A1 Bidding**	Collusion among bidders and executing agencies, and unmanaged conflict of interest	Conflicts of interest, fraud, and corruption jeopardizing the project and alienating prospective bidders
	A2 Bid evaluation	Inadequate due diligence, inconsistent application of bid evaluation criteria, and incorrect evaluation procedure and/or scoring	Diminished procurement's transparency and fairness resulting in awarding contracts to unqualified bidders
	A3 Contract award	Lack of standard contractual provisions to ensure the contractors' and subcontractors' accountability (e.g., audit, anticorruption, and records management clauses)	Inadequate audit trail thereby making any integrity violations, noncompliance, and other irregularities less detectable
Contract and asset management	**B1 Contract administration**	Faulty enforcement of liquidated damages	Uncompensated delays or losses caused by erring contractors or suppliers
	B2 Output monitoring	Deficiencies in the reporting of project's implementation progress	Diminished transparency resulting in implementation complications not being timely addressed
		Use of substandard materials and acceptance of works that were substandard, defective, or off specifications resulting from the inadequate monitoring of contractors by executing/implementing agencies and supervision consultants	Implementation delays, inferior quality of outputs, and cost overruns
Financial management	**C1 Expenditure management**	Ineligible, unsupported, or inaccurate expenditures being paid resulting from weakness in review and analysis of claims	Heightened opportunities for fraud resulting in potential loss of project funds
	C2 Financial reporting	Inadequate and unreliable accounting systems	Greater risk of not detecting integrity violations, noncompliance, or other irregularities
			Flawed project management decisions based on inaccurate financial information

Source: Office of Anticorruption and Integrity, Asian Development Bank.

APPENDIX   List of Proactive Integrity Reviews of Education Projects

Country	Project	PIR Report Issuance Date
Bangladesh	Skills for Employment Investment Program–Tranche 1	Dec 2019
Cambodia	Second Education Sector Development Project	Jul 2010
Indonesia	Polytechnics Education Development Project	Jun 2017 Feb 2020 *(follow-up)*
Lao People's Democratic Republic	Second Education Quality Improvement Project	Nov 2007
Mongolia	Third Education Development Project	Jan 2010
Myanmar	Equipping Youth for Employment Project	Aug 2020
Nepal	Earthquake Emergency Assistance Project	Nov 2019
Sri Lanka	Education for Knowledge Society Project	Jan 2013
	Secondary Education Modernization Project II	Jul 2010
Viet Nam	Upper Secondary Education Development Project	Jan 2009

PIR = proactive integrity review.

Note: Publication of full proactive integrity review reports started in 2008. Proactive integrity review reports prior to 2008 published on the Asian Development Bank website only contain report abstracts/summaries.

ADB placed on hold its assistance in Myanmar effective 1 February 2021.

Source: Office of Anticorruption and Integrity, Asian Development Bank.